D0229109

Northumberland
Schools Library
Service

3 0132 02402956 8	
Askews & Holts	Jan-2016
S822.33 WHITE	£9.99

USBORNE

World of Shakespeare
Picture Book

ROSIE DICKINS

SHAKESPEARE CONSULTANT: DR. PAUL EDMONDSON
HEAD OF RESEARCH AND KNOWLEDGE, THE SHAKESPEARE BIRTHPLACE TRUST

ILLUSTRATED BY GALIA BERNSTEIN AND DESIGNED BY NICOLA BUTLER

CONTENTS

When you see writing like this, it means it's a quote from Shakespeare or someone from his time.

USBORNE QUICKLINKS

To find out more about Shakespeare's life, times and works, go to the Usborne Quicklinks website at www.usborne.com/quicklinks and type in the keywords 'Shakespeare picture book'. Please read our internet safety guidelines at the Usborne Quicklinks website.

A Country Boy

WILLIAM SHAKESPEARE was born nearly 500 years ago in Stratford-upon-Avon, an old English market town surrounded by green fields and ancient woodlands. This is where he grew up, and where his family lived when he went to work in London.

Shakespeare was born in April 1564. According to tradition, he was born and died on April 23rd – St. George's Day. Shakespeare's father, John, was a glove-maker, wool-dealer and town councillor, and the family was quite well off.

SCHOOL

As a boy, Shakespeare went to the town's Grammar School, where he learned ancient Greek and Latin and studied ancient texts. Lessons started as early as 6am and lasted until evening, every day except Sunday – when everyone had to go to church.

SHAKESPEARE'S BIRTHPLACE
This is the house where Shakespeare was born. It is now a museum.

INSIDE THE GRAMMAR SCHOOL
Known as King Edward VI School, this is still a school today.

*The whining school-boy, with his satchel
And shining morning face, creeping like snail
Unwillingly to school.*

Shakespeare describes walking to school in *As You Like It*.

This is a horn-book (so called because the print is protected by a thin piece of horn). Shakespeare first learned to read from a horn-book just like this one.

NEXT STEPS

At 14, Shakespeare left school and helped his father with the family business. No one knows exactly how he got into plays, but he must have been inspired by the wandering players who visited Stratford from time to time.

ANNE HATHAWAY'S COTTAGE

On the outskirts of Stratford lies a pretty thatched cottage where Shakespeare's wife, Anne Hathaway, grew up. They married when Shakespeare was just 18 and Anne was 27, and had three children together.

ANNE HATHAWAY'S COTTAGE

Those lips that Love's own hand did make...

Sonnet 145

Shakespeare probably wrote one of his earliest love poems for Anne.

When Shakespeare died, he left Anne his second-best bed. This was their marriage bed (the best bed was used only for guests). Doing this gave Anne the right to stay on in their house, which he had left to their daughter.

NEW PLACE

By the time he was 33, Shakespeare had made enough money to buy New Place, the biggest house in central Stratford, for Anne and the children. He regularly spent time there, and died in New Place in April 1616.

NEW PLACE GARDENS

New Place no longer stands but you can still see its gardens, laid out in the style of Shakespeare's time.

SHAKESPEARE'S MEMORIAL

This memorial to Shakespeare – put up by his family – hangs above his grave in Holy Trinity Church.

The stone that marks Shakespeare's burial place has a warning carved into it.

Legend says Shakespeare died from a fever after a night out with his friends, including the playwright Ben Jonson.

GOOD FRIEND FOR JESUS' SAKE FORBEAR,
TO DIG THE DUST ENCLOSED HERE,
BLESSED BE THE MAN THAT SPARES THESE STONES,
AND CURSED BE HE THAT MOVES MY BONES.

HOLY TRINITY CHURCH
as it looks today

HOLY TRINITY CHURCH

Holy Trinity Church stands by the river in Stratford. Dating from 1210, it is the oldest building in the town. This is where ... were baptized, and where ... ried.

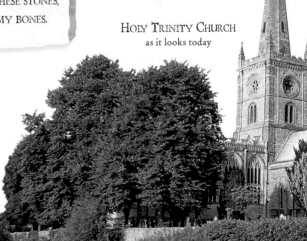

LONDON

Would I were in an alehouse in London!
A character in *Henry V*

TO SHAKESPEARE, London was the great city where he came to make his fortune as an actor and playwright. It was then a dirty, noisy, bustling place, home to around 200,000 people.

OLD ST PAUL'S, painted in 1616 by John Gipkin
This shows an open-air sermon beneath the tower.

OLD ST PAUL'S

The tower of Old St Paul's Cathedral towered over the city (until it burned down and was replaced by a domed building, which still stands today). St Paul's churchyard was full of booksellers and printers. It was here that Shakespeare's poems were first printed and sold.

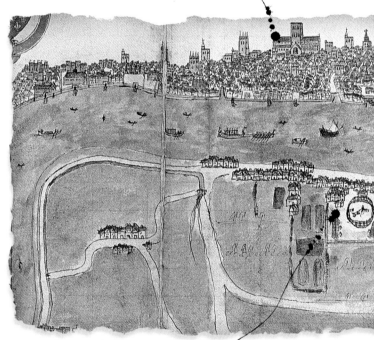

LONDON MAP, 1588

The playhouses changed their shows almost every day – meaning lots of work for an ambitious playwright and actor like Shakespeare.

STREETS

London street names often told you what you could find there. You could buy bread in Bread Street, milk in Milk Street and honey in Honey Lane, or order new clothes from the tailors in Threadneedle Street.

BEYOND THE LIMITS

There were strict controls on entertainments inside the city limits. So the playhouses clustered in seedy districts on the outskirts, alongside dog and bear-fighting pits, taverns, brothels and gambling dens.

OLD LONDON BRIDGE

This was the only bridge across the river in the city. It was a broad, stone bridge, built over with shops and houses. The end was guarded by a gatehouse and locked at night. Above the gate, the heads of rebels and traitors were displayed on spikes, as a grisly warning to those passing underneath.

FROST FAIR OF 1683-84, painted in 1685
In very cold weather, if the Thames froze, there would be ice-skating and 'frost fairs' like this, when market stalls and entertainments were set up on the ice. In the distance, you can see the arches of Old London Bridge.

THE RIVER THAMES

The River Thames connects London to the sea. In Shakespeare's day, it was busy with boats: sailing ships laden with exotic cargoes, ferries carrying ordinary people around, and fancy barges for the rich and powerful – including a grand golden one for the Queen.

The barge she sat in, like a burnished throne, Burned on the water.

Shakespeare describes a royal barge in *Antony and Cleopatra*.

DIRT AND DEATH

The city streets were awash with filth and human waste. In crowded, dirty conditions, disease was a constant threat. A disease known as the plague was especially deadly. Recurring outbreaks forced playhouses to close and killed Londoners by the thousand.

The streets were so smelly, people carried bottles or balls of perfume to ward off the stink.

PLAGUE SCENE, woodcut from 1625
This old woodcut shows a skeleton dancing on the coffins of plague victims and pleads: 'Lord have mercy on London.'

SHAKESPEARE'S TIME

IN SHAKESPEARE'S TIME, people thought quite differently about many things. Most people were much more religious and superstitious than today, and very loyal to the Queen, Elizabeth I.

RELIGION

Religion was a big part of life and you were fined if you didn't go to church. Christians were divided between Protestants and Catholics. England was officially Protestant, like the Queen. But some experts have suggested Shakespeare's family was secretly Catholic – risking punishment if they were found out.

QUEEN ELIZABETH AT PRAYER, painted in 1569
This prayerbook illustration shows the Protestant Queen kneeling devoutly.

Whatever his beliefs, Shakespeare can't have had much liking for the very strict Protestants known as Puritans. The Puritans thought plays were bad for people and campaigned to close all playhouses.

Dost thou think, because thou art virtuous, there shall be no more cakes and ale?

In Shakespeare's *Twelfth Night*, the jolly Sir Toby Belch mocks the Puritan Malvolio.

EXPLORING THE WORLD

The world still contained many unexplored places, but adventurers were starting to fill in the blanks. Sir Walter Raleigh sailed to the Americas in search of a fabled city of gold. And Sir Francis Drake sailed all the way around the world in his ship, *The Golden Hind*.

17TH-CENTURY
MODEL SAILING SHIP

MALVOLIO AND SIR TOBY BELCH
drawn in 1954 by Ronald Searle

SCIENCE AND MAGIC

The difference between science and magic was much less clear than today. Early scientists, known as alchemists, searched for a way of magically turning lead into gold. And astrologers studied the stars, believing they influenced events on earth.

ASTROLOGICAL CHART
Astrologers divided the skies into twelve sections, known as signs of the zodiac – as shown by this chart from a 16th-century map.

MEDICINE

Doctors believed your temperament and health were dictated by four bodily fluids, or 'humours': phlegm, blood, black bile and yellow bile. Any imbalance could lead to problems. For example, Shakespeare's character Hamlet was said to have too much black bile, which made him melancholy.

THE FOUR HUMOURS, drawn in 1574
This old book illustration shows a figure divided according to the humours.

WITCHES AND FAIRIES

Many people believed in witches and fairies, and Shakespeare included them in his plays. This was a serious matter – people accused of witchcraft (often old women who didn't fit in) could be executed if found guilty.

Double, double, toil and trouble; fire burn, and cauldron bubble...

The witches in *Macbeth* chant a spell.

FAIRIES FROM *A MIDSUMMER NIGHT'S DREAM* by William Blake
This painting, made about 1785, was inspired by Shakespeare.

SOCIAL ORDER

Society followed a strict pecking order, which Shakespeare called 'degree'. The king or queen came at the top, followed by nobles and churchmen, with ordinary folk below. Above the king and queen came the angels and eventually God hi‑‑‑‑‑‑ho was said to be the creator and ju‑‑‑

An Actor's Life

SHAKESPEARE PROBABLY GOT INTO WRITING through acting. In his day, it was normal for actors to help to write and adapt plays as they went along.

Wandering Players

Bands of wandering players journeyed from town to town, performing plays on makeshift stages. Shakespeare may have made his way to London with one of these bands.

ACTORS AT A VILLAGE FAIR
17th-century painting by Cornelis Beelt
This shows wandering players putting on a show.

Perils of Acting

By law, players had to have permits and a well-connected supporter or 'patron', but some people still looked down on acting as disreputable. All plays had to be approved by an official censor, who could shut down the playhouses if anyone disobeyed him.

Acting Companies

In London, Shakespeare and some fellow actors set up their own acting company, known as the Lord Chamberlain's Men. They even built their own playhouse, named the Globe.

The Globe was a round, wooden building.

All the world's a stage,
And all the men and women merely players:
They have their exits and their entrances;
And one man in his time plays many parts.

A character in *As You Like It* compares life to acting.

Kemps nine daies vvonder.

Performed in a daunce from London to Norwich.

Containing the pleasure, paines and kinde entertainment of William Kemp betweene London and that City in his late Morrice.

Wherein is somewhat set downe worth note; to reprooue the slaunders spred of him many things merry, nothing hurtfull.

Written by himselfe to satisfie his friends.

LONDON,
and are to be
of Saint

Stars of the Stage

The Lord Chamberlain's Men included Richard Burbage, a renowned actor and one of the biggest stars of his day, and Will Kemp, a popular clown. Shakespeare wrote many roles specifically for them.

WILL KEMP, woodcut from 1600
Thi[s] [shows Kem]p dancing. Kemp loved showing [off. He dance]d all the way from London to [Norwich as a publ]icity stunt.

RICHARD BURBAGE, 17th-century painting
Burbage was the first person to play many famous Shakespeare characters, including Hamlet, Romeo and Macbeth.

PROMPT BOOK

One of a company's most valuable possessions was the 'prompt book' containing their plays. Often, this was the *only* copy of the plays, guarded jealously so no one else could perform them.

Some of Shakespeare's plays were printed during his life, but half were only published after his death, when two of his friends produced an official collection.

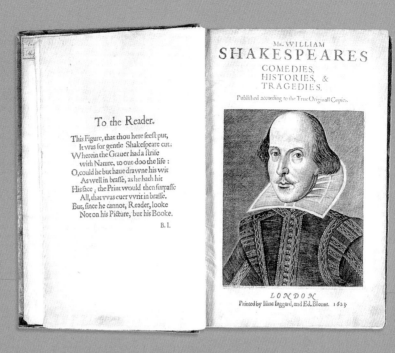

To the Reader.

This Figure, that thou here seest put,
It was for gentle Shakespeare cut;
Wherein the Grauer had a strife
with Nature, to out-doo the life :
O, could he but haue drawne his wit
As well in brasse, as he hath hit
His face ; the Print would then surpasse
All, that vvas euer vvrit in brasse.
But, since he cannot, Reader, looke
Not on his Picture, but his Booke.
B. I.

Mr. WILLIAM
SHAKESPEARES
COMEDIES,
HISTORIES, &
TRAGEDIES.
Published according to the True Originall Copies.

LONDON
Printed by Isaac Iaggard, and Ed. Blount. 1623.

FIRST FOLIO, 1623
This was the first official collection of Shakespeare's plays, published by two friends trying to preserve his memory.

It contains one of the best-known pictures of Shakespeare.

STAGING A PLAY

Plays were staged with few props and no scenery – the setting was left to the audience's imagination. But actors did wear extravagant silk and velvet costumes. They had music and special effects, too. Actors might use pigs' blood for gory sword fights, appear and disappear through trapdoors, or 'fly' using ropes.

In Shakespeare's day, actors wore the fashions of their own time, even when a play was set in the past.

Wig

Ruff

This jacket was known as a doublet.

PLAYING WOMEN
Women were not allowed to act in public. So women's parts were taken by boys or young men whose voices hadn't broken yet.

Above the stage was a canopy known as the 'heavens'. Trapdoors in the floor led down to an understage area known as 'hell'.

MAKING IT BIG

SHAKESPEARE'S PLAYS were popular with everyone from the ordinary folk who filled the playhouses, to wealthy nobles who hired his company to put on private performances for them and their friends.

One penny was the price of admission.

An upstart crow...
in his own conceit the only
Shake-scene in a country

Shakespeare's success provoked jealousy from other playwrights.

PLAYHOUSE CROWDS

Huge crowds flocked to the playhouses to see Shakespeare's plays. As many as 3,000 people might crowd in for a single show – from the 'groundlings' who stood in the yard to wealthier playgoers with seats in the galleries.

ACTING A SHAKESPEARE PLAY
This 19th-century print shows how a playhouse might have looked in Shakespeare's day, with groundlings crowding around the stage.

ROYAL ENTERTAINMENT

Shakespeare's company, the Lord Chamberlain's Men, performed for the Queen several times, as part of lavish court entertainments. The Queen's love of plays was one reason the playhouses stayed open, despite attempts from Puritans and others to close them down.

QUEEN ELIZABETH I, painted about 1580 by Nicholas Hilliard
The Queen loved music, poetry and plays. This miniature portrait shows her playing a stringed instrument known as a lute.

HENRY CAREY, painted in 1576
Patron of Shakespeare's company

LORD PATRON

Shakespeare's company took their name from their first patron, the Lord Chamberlain Henry Carey. As the Lord Chamberlain, he was in charge of the Queen's entertainments – so he had the right connections to help their careers.

THE KING'S MEN

When King James I came to the throne, he asked Shakespeare's company to become the King's Men. The renamed company performed many times for the new king. Since James was Scottish and was interested in witches, Shakespeare wrote *Macbeth,* a Scottish play with witches in it, especially to please him.

KING JAMES I, painted in 1610-11 by Nicholas Hilliard
This jewel-encrusted miniature portrait was made to be worn like a locket. The front shows James's initial and the letter 'R' for *Rex*, which means 'king' in Latin.

James took a special interest in witches after he was nearly shipwrecked in a storm blamed on witchcraft.

THE GREAT HALL AT HAMPTON COURT PALACE, painted about 1838
Shakespeare's company put on several plays for James in this enormous palace hall soon after he became king.

Some are born great, some achieve greatness, and some have greatness thrust upon them.

A servant in *Twelfth Night* talks about success.

FAME AND FORTUNE

Shakespeare didn't just find fame but fortune, too. He was good with money and, by the time of his death, owned a large amount of property in London and Stratford. His family was even given a coat of arms.

NON SANZ DROICT

The coat of arms includes a golden spear, in reference to Shakespeare's name. The Latin motto below means: 'Not without right'.

WILLIAM SHAKESPEARE

LASTING FAME

After Shakespeare's death, his fame continued to grow. Today, there are memorials to him all over the world.

SHAKESPEARE MEMORIAL, POETS' CORNER
The most famous English writers are commemorated in Poets' Corner inside Westminster Abbey, London. A memorial to Shakespeare was put up there in 1740.

THE GLOBE

SHAKESPEARE'S OWN PLAYHOUSE, the Globe, stood on the south bank of the River Thames in London. In its heyday, it was known as 'the glorie of the Banke'. Today a replica Globe stands on almost the same spot.

A flag was raised, and a trumpet blown, to announce the start of a play.

The Globe was a round, wooden building with an open-air stage in the middle. There was no lighting, so plays had to finish before dusk.

A penny bought you standing room in the yard. Two pence bought a seat in a gallery.

Playgoers would shout, whistle and even throw things if they didn't like something.

In hot weather, groundlings were also known as 'stinkards'.

The balcony was mostly used by musicians, but it was also used for balcony scenes.

The doors at the back of the stage led to the 'tiring house' where actors could change their costumes.

Nuts were a popular snack with playgoers and the floor of the yard crunched underfoot with discarded shells.

This wooden O
Shakespeare describes the playhouse in *Henry V*.

STOLEN TIMBERS
The Globe was built in 1599 from the timbers of another playhouse. Shakespeare's company dismantled the old playhouse and rebuilt it on a new site after having problems with their landlord.

EVIDENCE

There are no surviving pictures of the inside of the Globe. But we know roughly how it looked from written descriptions and sketches of other playhouses, and studies of the ground where it stood.

THE SWAN in 1596
This shows the inside of another London playhouse, as sketched by a visitor.

FIRE

The Globe was built of wood, with a thatched roof. In 1613, a spark from a cannon used in a play set fire to the thatch and the playhouse burned to the ground. No one was hurt, although one man's breeches caught fire and had to be put out with beer.

Totus mundus agit histrionem

Legend has it this Latin motto was inscribed over the entrance to the Globe. It means 'the whole world plays the actor' – an idea echoed by Shakespeare's line, 'All the world's a stage.'

THE END...

After the fire, the Globe was quickly rebuilt, this time with a tiled roof. The new Globe ran until 1642, when Puritans banned all plays. The building was torn down soon after. The ban on plays was lifted in 1660, but the Globe was gone for good – or so it seemed.

...AND A NEW BEGINNING

In the 1970s, actor and director Sam Wanamaker determined to rebuild the lost playhouse. After a long struggle, the replica, known as Shakespeare's Globe, opened in 1997. It is a round wooden building, built on almost the same spot, and as closely as possible to the original.

THE GLOBE
An 18th-century artist's impression

SHAKESPEARE'S GLOBE TODAY
This is the building you see today. Notice the timber frame. The timbers were cut from English oak, which is famously strong. The roof is thatched with reeds – although unlike the original, it has fire retardants and sprinklers.

Inside, playgoers stand in the yard or sit in galleries, just as they would have done in Shakespeare's day – although modern safety regulations limit the number to 1,500, about half the original audience.

Making History

SHAKESPEARE'S FIRST HIT was a play about an English king, Henry VI. He followed it up with more plays about English history – but had to be careful how he presented it...

CHOOSING THE RED AND WHITE ROSES by Henry Payne
This painting from 1910 – inspired by Shakespeare – shows bands of rivals picking red or white roses to show which side they supported in the Wars of the Roses.

WARS OF THE ROSES

Shakespeare's history plays mostly describe events from the Wars of the Roses, a time of bitter struggle between branches of England's royal family. The plays also celebrate the rise to power of Queen Elizabeth's branch of the family, the Tudors.

The Tudor symbol was a red and white rose – symbolizing the union of the warring sides.

MAN OR MONSTER?

The first Tudor king, Henry VII, came to power by deposing the previous king, Richard III. Shakespeare's Richard is a deformed, murderous monster, making Henry look like a hero. In fact, Richard was known in his time as a skilled military leader and just lawmaker.

HOW ACCURATE?

Shakespeare's version of history isn't always reliable. He was more interested in telling a good story than getting the facts exactly right. And he had to avoid offending the current Tudor queen.

that bottled spider, that foul hunchbacked toad
Shakespeare describes Richard III.

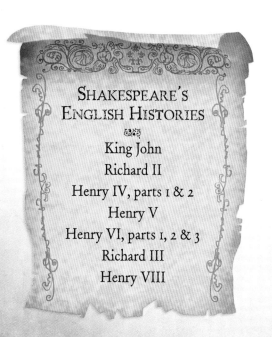

SHAKESPEARE'S ENGLISH HISTORIES

King John
Richard II
Henry IV, parts 1 & 2
Henry V
Henry VI, parts 1, 2 & 3
Richard III
Henry VIII

RICHARD III
by an unknown 15th-century artist
This is how the king looked in a portrait made during his lifetime...

...but in Shakespeare's play, he has a hunched back, withered arm and limp.

Kevin Spacey as RICHARD III
on stage in 2011

14

FIGHTING SPIRIT

The play Henry V celebrates the English king's famous victory over the French at the Battle of Agincourt. Shakespeare wrote such stirring, patriotic speeches that the play was made into a movie during the Second World War, to encourage British audiences to support their country.

Laurence Olivier as HENRY V

This is a still from the wartime movie of *Henry V*. The movie, made in 1944, was dedicated to the 'Commandos and Airborne Troops of Great Britain'.

THE BATTLE OF AGINCOURT, 1415
This illustration, by an unknown 15th-century artist, pictures the English forces overcoming the French.

We few, we happy few, we band of brothers;
For he today that sheds his blood with me
Shall be my brother.

Henry V rallies his troops before battle.

The English soldiers used longbows, which gave them a huge advantage over the French troops.

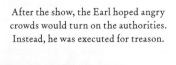

DANGEROUS GROUND

Writing and performing plays about history could be dangerous. In *Richard II*, Shakespeare included a scene where rebels depose the king. The censor stopped the scene from being printed – but it still led to trouble...

Hoping to start a rebellion, the Earl of Essex paid Shakespeare's company to stage a special performance of *Richard II*. The plan failed. The actors apologized and were pardoned by the Queen – but the Earl was sent to the Tower of London.

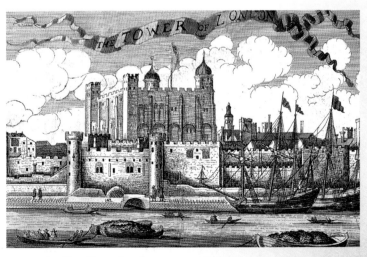

THE TOWER OF LONDON in an engraving made about 1700
The Tower is one of the oldest buildings in London and stands largely unchanged to this day. Many traitors have been locked up and beheaded there, including the Earl of Essex in 1601.

After the show, the Earl hoped angry crowds would turn on the authorities. Instead, he was executed for treason.

COMEDIES

SHAKESPEARE'S COMEDIES are among his most popular plays. Full of sparkling romance and knockabout jokes, they still thrill audiences today.

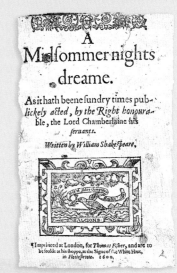

A Midsommer nights dreame.

As it hath beene sundry times pub-lickely acted, by the Right honoura-ble, the Lord Chamberlaine his servants.

Written by William Shakespeare.

An early printed edition of one of Shakespeare's most famous comedies

MAGIC AND MAYHEM

Most of the comedies focus on young lovers overcoming hardships, from family arguments and jealous rivals to shipwrecks and separation – with a lot of comic confusion and witty wordplay along the way.

A mischievous fairy, Puck, causes magical mayhem.

Lord, what fools these mortals be!

Puck laughs at human lovers in *A Midsummer Night's Dream.*

HAPPY ENDINGS

Although these plays are comedies, they aren't funny all of the time. Difficult things do happen and not everyone gets what they want. But the characters don't suffer for long and there is always a happy ending – usually with the main characters getting married.

PUCK, drawn in 1908 by Arthur Rackham

The rain it raineth every day.

Twelfth Night

Melancholy songs often help to balance the comedy.

SHAKESPEARE'S COMEDIES

Two Gentlemen of Verona

The Comedy of Errors

Love's Labour's Lost

A Midsummer Night's Dream

The Merry Wives of Windsor

Much Ado About Nothing

As You Like It

Twelfth Night

Argumentative lovers Beatrice and Benedick embrace at the end of a 1993 movie of Much Ado About Nothing.

LIGHT AND DARK

Not all of Shakespeare's comedies are as light-hearted as the ones described here, or follow the same pattern. Some, often known as 'problem plays', have a darker side (see page 18). Others, written later in Shakespeare's life, are more like magical adventure stories (see page 26).

TWELFTH NIGHT

This tangled story has a lovesick duke wooing a reclusive lady. But the lady prefers the duke's serving boy – while the 'boy' (a girl in disguise) pines for the duke. More confusion is caused by mischievous servants and a lost twin. But it all finishes happily, with a triple wedding.

If music be the food of love, play on...

In the opening lines of *Twelfth Night*,
the duke calls for music while he talks about love.

Stephen Fry plays Malvolio, one of the servants, on stage in 2012. Malvolio has been tricked into thinking the lady loves *him*, and puts on yellow stockings to impress her.

TITANIA AND BOTTOM, a 19th-century painting by John Fitzgerald
In *A Midsummer Night's Dream*, magic makes the fairy queen, Titania,
fall madly in love with an actor named Bottom – who has
magically been given a donkey's head.

A MIDSUMMER NIGHT'S DREAM

In this enchanting play, fairy magic makes two pairs of runaway lovers fall in and out of love with each other. Meanwhile, a group of amateur actors rehearses an amusingly awful play. It ends with the lovers reunited, their weddings blessed by their families and the fairies.

A small fairy waits upon her queen.

What angel wakes me from my flowery bed?

When Bottom brays like a donkey,
Titania thinks he sounds like an angel.

AS YOU LIKE IT

When her wicked uncle usurps the throne, Rosalind runs away to the forest, disguised as a boy, to look for her exiled father. There, quarrels are made up, families are brought back together, and Rosalind finds true love.

Under the greenwood tree
Who loves to lie with me...
Here shall he see
No enemy
But winter and rough weather.

Song from *As You Like It*

ROSALIND IN THE FOREST, painted about 1868
by John Everett Millais

PROBLEM PLAYS

A FEW SHAKESPEARE PLAYS, often called 'problem plays' by critics, don't really fit any category. In some ways they seem like comedies. But they also introduce darker elements which are never quite dealt with.

DARK TIMES

Critics disagree over the term 'problem play' and what Shakespeare may have meant when he wrote them. Certainly the plays don't encourage neat definitions. But they do all share an awkward atmosphere. Lovers prove unfaithful, heroes don't succeed and marriages are unhappy.

TROILUS AND CRESSIDA
(Stage performance from 2008) Against a backdrop of war and betrayal, a young couple promise to love each other forever – but it doesn't last.

SHAKESPEARE'S PROBLEM PLAYS
*
The Merchant of Venice
Troilus and Cressida
Measure for Measure
All's Well That Ends Well

WHAT'S THE PROBLEM?

Some people believe Shakespeare was prompted to write the problem plays by troubles in his own life. Others think he was experimenting. And some claim these aren't really problem plays at all, but comedies written at a time when life could be much more harsh.

GREEK VASE WITH SCENE OF THE TROJAN WAR
This 2,500-year-old vase depicts the same war which inspired *Troilus and Cressida*.

ALL'S WELL THAT ENDS WELL?

The problem plays make a mockery of traditional happy endings. For example, in *All's Well That Ends Well*, Helena wins the hand of the man she loves, only for him to run away. She wins him back through trickery, but he remains a reluctant husband – begging the question: is all really well that ends 'well'?

ALL'S WELL THAT ENDS WELL
(Stage performance from 2009) Although the main characters end up married, the love is all on one side.

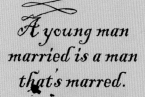

A young man married is a man that's marred.

A young man in *All's Well That Ends Well* protests against marriage.

RIGHT OR WRONG?

Two famously problematic plays, *Measure for Measure* and *The Merchant of Venice*, both address issues of justice in a murky, complicated world.

CLAUDIO AND ISABELLA
painted in 1850 by William Holman Hunt
Isabella tries to comfort her brother, Claudio, who has been sentenced to death by Angelo (although he is eventually freed).

MEASURE FOR MEASURE

Angelo is left in charge of a city by his master, ordering executions and trying to take advantage of the pious Isabella, while abandoning his fiancée. When the duke returns, Angelo is forced to marry his fiancée, while the duke proposes to Isabella – but there is no sense of a happy ever after.

*Oh it is excellent
To have a giant's strength; but it is tyrannous
To use it like a giant.*

Isabella pleads with Angelo for her brother's life.

THE MERCHANT OF VENICE
painted about 1900 by Christian August Printz

THE MERCHANT OF VENICE

Antonio borrows some money to help his friend, Bassanio, woo the beautiful Portia. In exchange, Antonio promises to repay the loan or give the lender, Shylock, a pound of his own flesh. When the time comes, he cannot repay it – but Portia comes to his rescue. Disguised as a lawyer, she goes to court and argues that Shylock may take only flesh, not blood, forcing him to spare Antonio.

THE MERCHANT OF VENICE
In one scene, Bassanio has to choose between three caskets – each engraved with a promise or a warning – to win Portia's hand in marriage. He correctly chooses one made of lead, rather than glittering gold or silver.

WHO CHOOSES ME SHALL GAIN WHAT MANY MEN DESIRE

WHO CHOOSES ME SHALL GET AS MUCH AS HE DESERVES

WHO CHOOSES ME MUST GIVE AND HAZARD ALL HE HAS

If you prick us, do we not bleed?

Shylock argues that Jews deserve to be treated like other people, not persecuted.

VICTIM OR VILLAIN?

Shylock is a difficult character to judge. He is horribly cruel to Antonio. But he has also suffered awful abuse from Antonio, because he is a Jew. Is he victim or villain? There is no easy answer.

19

POEMS

SHAKESPEARE'S FIRST PUBLISHED WORKS were poems –
considered the most noble form of writing at the time.

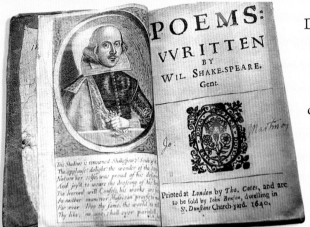

This early copy
of Shakespeare's
poems dates
from 1640.

LONG POEMS

During his life, Shakespeare published two long poems
inspired by love and classical literature. They include
his first published work, *Venus and Adonis*, a poem
based on an ancient Greek myth. He also wrote a
collection of short poems known as sonnets, from the
Italian word *sonetto,* which means 'little sound'.

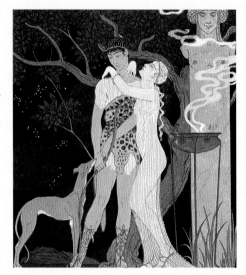

VENUS AND ADONIS
painted in the 1920s by Georges Barbier
Venus was the Greek goddess of love.
According to myth, she fell in love with
a handsome huntsman named Adonis.

PATRONS

Shakespeare dedicated his long poems to his
patron, Henry Wriothesley, Earl of Southampton.
In return, the Earl gave him money and support.
Some people think Shakespeare's sonnets –
which were dedicated to a mysterious
'Mr. W. H.' – were meant for the Earl, too.

Shakespeare probably turned to poetry
to make a living in years when the London
playhouses were closed due to plague.

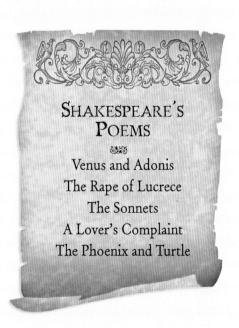

EARL OF SOUTHAMPTON
painted about 1594 by Nicholas Hilliard
This miniature portrait shows
Shakespeare's patron, Henry
Wriothesley, who had poems and books
dedicated to him by several writers.

The playhouses had to close when plague
deaths rose above 30 a week. Some doctors
wore masks to try to protect themselves.

SHAKESPEARE'S POEMS

Venus and Adonis
The Rape of Lucrece
The Sonnets
A Lover's Complaint
The Phoenix and Turtle

SONNETS

A sonnet is a 14-line poem. Collections of love sonnets were very fashionable in Shakespeare's time. Shakespeare wrote 154 sonnets. Some are addressed to men, some to women, but most are universal and are about the many moods of love, fame, time, old age and even writing itself.

Shall I compare thee to a summer's day?
Thou art more lovely and more temperate.
Rough winds do shake the darling buds of May,
And summer's lease hath all too short a date.

The opening lines of one of Shakespeare's most famous sonnets (no. 18) compare his beloved to the beauty of summer.

MINIATURE PORTRAIT OF A LADY
painted in 1593 by Nicholas Hilliard
Shakespeare's sonnets are often compared to miniature portraits, like this one, which were also popular at the time. Both sonnets and miniatures were small and delicately crafted, and intended for a small audience.

REAL PEOPLE?

Many readers have tried, unsuccessfully, to identify real people from Shakespeare's life in the sonnets. The poems do seem written from the heart, but that is the skill of the poet. It doesn't mean Shakespeare lived through everything he describes.

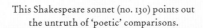

My mistress' eyes are nothing like the sun...

This Shakespeare sonnet (no. 130) points out the untruth of 'poetic' comparisons.

BREAKING THE RULES

Most sonnets were polite love poems that followed a particular pattern of rhymes. But Shakespeare broke the rules, tinkering with the pattern and making fun of the exaggerated comparisons used by other poets.

ROMEO AND JULIET
19th-century painting by Jennie Harbour
Romeo and Juliet fall in love at first sight.

POEMS AND PLAYS

Sonnets are so good at conveying feelings, Shakespeare also used them in his plays. For example, when the famous lovers Romeo and Juliet meet for the very first time, their words to each other combine to form a sonnet – immediately conjuring up a feeling of romance.

Shakespeare's sonnets have inspired many other writers and performers. This photograph shows an actor playing Queen Elizabeth I in a musical version, called *Shakespeare's Sonnette*, from 2009.

LOVE AND DEATH

SHAKESPEARE'S MOST FAMOUS PLAYS are his tragedies. Packed with blood, guts, intrigue and passion, they contain some of his most powerful writing and many of his most memorable characters.

UNHAPPY ENDINGS

Some of Shakespeare's tragedies are about doomed love; others explore kingship and power (see page 24). All show people suffering and struggling to overcome events. But something – whether fate or a fatal flaw in their character – always dooms them to fail. So things end badly, leaving the stage littered with corpses.

About ten Shakespeare plays are usually described as tragedies. But he also mixed elements of tragedy into his history plays and comedies, so not everyone agrees on an exact list.

ROMEO AND JULIET, painted in 1868-71 by Ford Madox Brown
Romeo climbs up onto Juliet's balcony to visit her in secret.

BALLET OF
ROMEO AND JULIET
(performance from 2009)
Shakespeare's tragic love story has inspired many retellings, including a ballet, an opera and several movies.

ROMEO AND JULIET

This is one of Shakespeare's earliest tragedies. Romeo and Juliet come from warring families; they fall in love and secretly marry. Then Romeo is forced to flee and Juliet, threatened by a new suitor, fakes her own death. Believing she really is dead, Romeo kills himself in despair. Then, when Juliet discovers his body, she kills herself too.

For never was a story of more woe
Than this of Juliet and her Romeo.

Last line of *Romeo and Juliet*

SHAKESPEARE'S TRAGEDIES

Titus Andronicus	Timon of Athens
Romeo and Juliet	King Lear
Julius Caesar	Macbeth
Hamlet	Antony and Cleopatra
Othello	Coriolanus

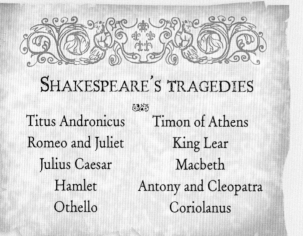

OTHELLO

This is a dark play about love, jealousy and racism. Othello, a black general, marries Desdemona, a white lady. A jealous fellow soldier then tricks Othello into believing Desdemona has been unfaithful. Crazed with jealousy, Othello murders her. Then, when he discovers his mistake, he kills himself.

Othello listens reluctantly to accusations against his wife, in a stage performance from 2007.

Put out the light, and then put out the light.

Othello talks to himself as he enters Desdemona's bedroom to kill her.

KING LEAR

Old King Lear demands his daughters say how much they love him. Cordelia, who truly loves him, cannot find the words and is banished. Her sisters speak prettily, but prove treacherous. Shakespeare borrowed the fairytale formula from an old English folk tale, but there is no fairytale ending. In his play, Lear and his three daughters all die.

CORDELIA COMFORTING KING LEAR IN PRISON, painted in 1886 by George Joy
Lear and Cordelia are reunited in prison, before Cordelia is executed by their enemies. The old king then dies of grief.

If you think King Lear is too sad, you wouldn't be alone. For well over a hundred years, the play was only performed in a rewritten version, in which Lear is restored to the throne and Cordelia survives.

ANTONY AND CLEOPATRA

In this doomed love story, Roman general Mark Antony has a passionate affair with Cleopatra, Queen of Egypt. Then the Roman army comes after him, there is a sea battle and Mark Antony loses. Believing Cleopatra dead, he stabs himself. She then kills herself rather than surrender.

Cleopatra kills herself by letting a poisonous snake bite her.

CLEOPATRA
This stone carving, made in Egypt over 2,000 years ago, shows how the real queen may have looked.

TRAGIC KINGS

SHAKESPEARE'S GREATEST TRAGEDIES include several plays which focus on kingship and power, and the awful things that can happen when power is abused.

HAMLET

Hamlet is one of Shakespeare's most popular, most performed plays. It tells the story of Hamlet, a young Danish prince, whose uncle usurps the throne by murdering Hamlets's father and marrying his mother. Hamlet meets his father's ghost and promises revenge, but finds it hard to decide what to do.

THE Tragicall Historie of HAMLET Prince of Denmarke
By William Shake-speare.

As it hath beene diuerse times acted by his Highnesse seruants in the Cittie of London : as also in the two Vniuersities of Cambridge and Oxford, and else-where

At London printed for N.L. and Iohn Trundell. 1603.

Title page of an early edition of *Hamlet*, Shakespeare's longest play, which takes around four hours to perform in full.

David Tennant as HAMLET on stage in 2008.

To be or not to be, that is the question.

In one famous speech, Hamlet wonders about killing himself as a solution to his troubles.

OPHELIA, painted in 1852 by Arthur Hughes
Ophelia, Hamlet's girlfriend, goes insane after Hamlet kills her father, and drowns while picking flowers.

CRAZY MINDS

Hamlet appears crazy at times, and his girlfriend Ophelia loses her reason and drowns herself – and they are not alone. In many of Shakespeare's tragedies, people go insane as their world falls apart. Yet often it is these characters who see through convention and speak the truth.

TAKING REVENGE

Shakespeare's tragedies form part of a tradition of bloodthirsty dramas known as revenge plays. These combine murder, ghosts, intrigue and insanity to melodramatic effect, usually leaving hardly anyone alive by the end.

Hamlet ends with Hamlet, his mother, his uncle and his girlfriend's brother all dying on stage.

Macbeth

Macbeth is such a dark, haunting play, some superstitious actors refuse to mention it by name. It tells of the rise and fall of an ambitious lord named Macbeth. Urged on by witches and a ruthless wife, he commits murder after murder – first to steal the throne, then as he tries (and fails) to hold onto it. By the end, he and most of the main characters are dead.

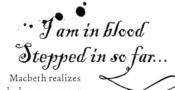

I am in blood Stepped in so far...
Macbeth realizes he has no way out.

MACBETH POSTER, created in 1911
This play poster features the famous scene where Macbeth meets the witches and they hail him as a future king – helping to set in motion a horrifying train of events.

Julius Caesar

Based on real events in ancient Rome, this tragedy tells the story of the Roman dictator, Julius Caesar, and his murder by a group of politicians – including Caesar's own friend, Brutus – after they feared he was becoming too powerful.

JULIUS CAESAR, a 19th-century painting by Vincenzo Camuccini
This pictures the moment of the assassination, when the politicians turned on Caesar and stabbed him 23 times.

Et tu, Brute? Then fall, Caesar!
Caesar asks (in Latin) 'You too, Brutus?' before giving himself up to his fate.

Dangerous questions

Shakespeare could write about dangerous questions, such as a leader's right to rule and the possibility of rebellion, more openly by setting his play firmly in the distant past.

On the back of the coin, daggers refer to the murder and le... ...des' (15th) of March.

LATE PLAYS

TOWARDS THE END OF HIS LIFE, Shakespeare began to write a new kind of comedy, creating plays with a miraculous, magical feeling to them.

HAPPY EVER AFTER

Shakespeare's early comedies were mostly about couples falling in love and getting married. The late plays are more like magical adventure stories and focus on families. They also mix up theatrical styles, drawing on tragedy, fantasy and romance as much as comedy. After many plot twists and turns, everyone is reunited and the villains are forgiven.

SHIPWRECK FROM THE TEMPEST
painted in 1908 by Edmund Dulac
The late plays are full of storms and shipwrecks, stressing people's helplessness in the face of nature.

SHAKESPEARE'S LATE PLAYS

Pericles
The Winter's Tale
Cymbeline
The Tempest

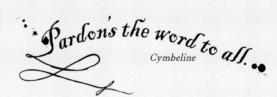

Pardon's the word to all.
Cymbeline

THE WINTER'S TALE

The Winter's Tale begins like a tragedy. Convinced his wife has been unfaithful, a king rejects his wife and baby girl. He soon realizes he was wrong, only to be told his wife has died. Sixteen years pass before the second half picks up the story, bringing the family back together with a series of magical coincidences.

These paintings show the contrast between the two halves of the play.

The king orders the baby to be left in the wild. The man who takes her is chased by a bear – giving rise to a famous stage direction – while the baby is rescued by a passing shepherd.

Some early performances may have used a real bear.

THE WINTER'S TALE, painted in 1790 by Joseph Wright

The lost girl, named Perdita by the shepherd, grows up in the countryside and finds love with a young prince named Florizel.

Exit, pursued by a bear.
Stage direction in *The Winter's Tale*

FLORIZEL AND PERDITA
20th-century painting by Mary Bank

THE TEMPEST

This magical tale tells how an exiled duke, Prospero, finds freedom and his daughter, Miranda, finds love with a shipwrecked prince. Also a powerful magician, Prospero summons storms, spirits and visions to carry out his orders. But once old wrongs have been righted, he gives up magic and forgives his enemies.

MIRANDA, painted in 1916 by John William Waterhouse
Kind-hearted Miranda sees a ship in trouble and begs Prospero to help the people on board – not knowing he raised the storm to fetch it.

Ralph Fiennes plays Prospero on stage in 2011.
The staff in his hand is a symbol of Prospero's magic.

Where the bee sucks there suck I...
On the bat's back I do fly...
A fairy song, sung by Ariel
in *The Tempest*

The isle is full of noises,
Sounds and sweet airs, that give
delight and hurt not.
In *The Tempest*, Caliban tells the shipwrecked men not to be afraid of the magical sounds they hear.

ARIEL
engraving from
about 1890
by Henry Selous

FAIRIES AND MONSTERS

Prospero has two servants, a fairy spirit named Ariel, and brutish, bad-tempered Caliban, who complains of being treated like a slave and plots against his master. But despite this, they both find happy endings, with Prospero giving them their freedom.

A FINAL FAREWELL

Prospero's power to control people and conjure up visions is often compared to Shakespeare's power as a writer. So when Prospero breaks his staff and renounces magic, it can also be seen as Shakespeare's farewell to the p̶l̶a̶y̶s. After this, he wrote no more major plays, though he did ̶w̶i̶t̶h̶ younger writers

A MAN FOR ALL TIME

SHAKESPEARE DIED OVER 400 YEARS AGO, but his plays are still enormously popular and are performed regularly all over the world.

This photograph is from a production of *King Lear* performed with traditional Indian costumes and music.

FINDING NEW AUDIENCES

Shakespeare's works have been translated into over 80 languages, from Arabic to Zulu. They have been turned into movies, operas and ballets, and adapted for different audiences, using a huge variety of costumes and settings.

SOME OF SHAKESPEARE'S INVENTIONS

blinking idiot
dead as a doornail
eaten out of house and home
for ever and a day
haven't slept a wink
laughing stock
one fell swoop
quick as a flash
tower of strength
wild-goose chase

THRONE OF BLOOD
This advertising poster was made for *Throne of Blood*, a 1957 Japanese movie based on *Macbeth*.

MIRROR TO NATURE

What has made Shakespeare appeal to so many people through the ages? Perhaps it is the way he creates lively characters dealing with familiar issues – love, families, power, intrigue, death – without taking sides. People often say his plays hold a 'mirror up to nature', leaving actors and audiences free to find their own meanings.

Shakespeare had at least six different ways of spelling his own name.

SHAKESPEARE'S LANGUAGE

When Shakespeare was writing, dictionaries hadn't been invented and language was much more changeable than it is today. Shakespeare had a huge influence in shaping how modern English developed, coining hundreds of new words and phrases.

TRY IT YOURSELF

Shakespeare's creative way with words included insults. Here, you can create your own Shakespearean insults choosing one from each speech bubble.

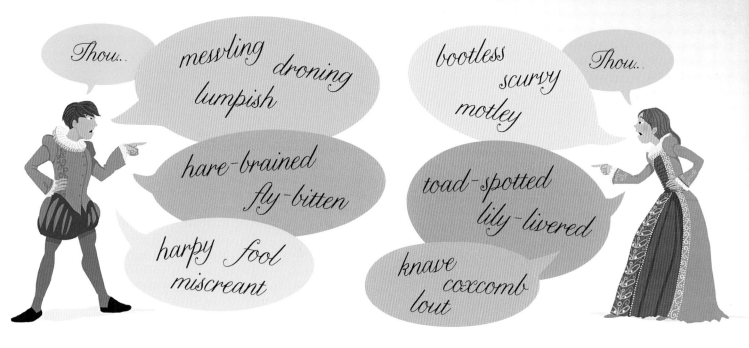

REMEMBERING SHAKESPEARE

In 1769, a famous actor named David Garrick set up the first Shakespeare festival in Stratford, with a costumed procession, dancing and fireworks. Today, the town continues to celebrate Shakespeare's birthday every year, and there are regular festivals of his plays around the world.

A ticket to Garrick's Shakespeare festival

WHAT WE DON'T KNOW

Shakespeare lived so long ago that there are many gaps in his life story – although that is quite usual for people of his time. Half his plays exist in more than one version, and there are thought to be two lost plays: *Love's Labour's Won* and *Cardenio*. But even though there is so much we don't know, he is still acknowledged as one of the world's greatest writers.

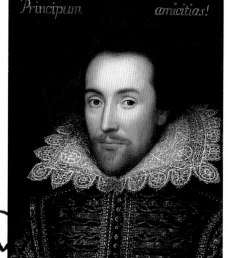

SHAKESPEARE?
The best-known portraits of Shakespeare were created after his death. Some experts think this picture – recently rediscovered – is a portrait made during his life, but others disagree.

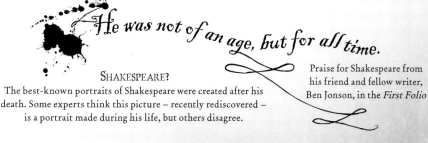

He was not of an age, but for all time.

Praise for Shakespeare from his friend and fellow writer, Ben Jonson, in the *First Folio*

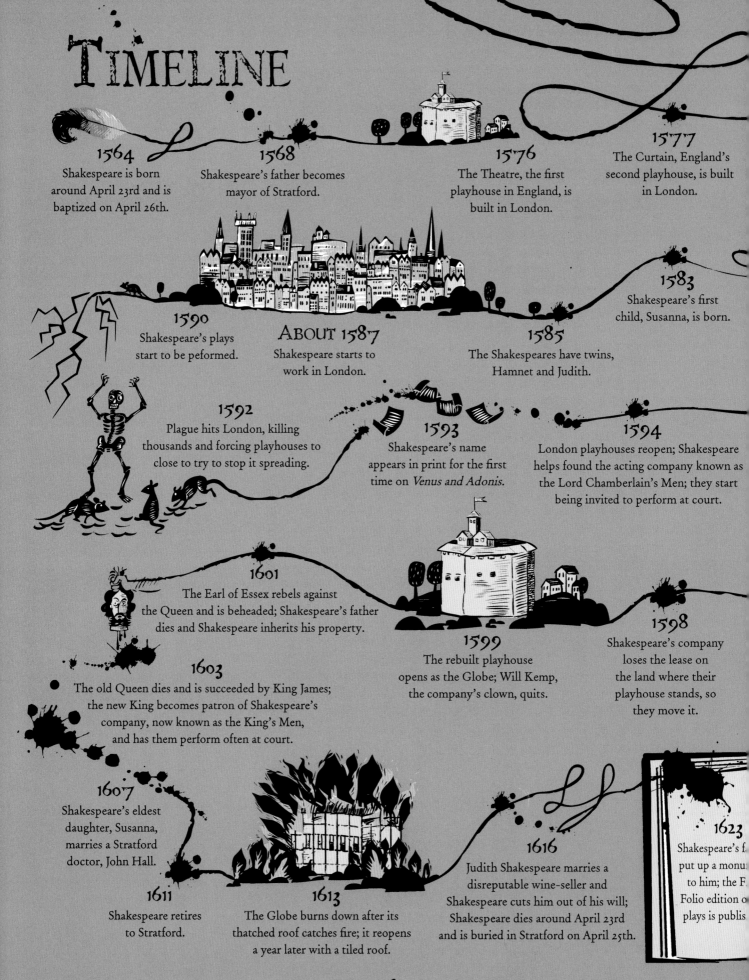

TIMELINE

1564
Shakespeare is born around April 23rd and is baptized on April 26th.

1568
Shakespeare's father becomes mayor of Stratford.

1576
The Theatre, the first playhouse in England, is built in London.

1577
The Curtain, England's second playhouse, is built in London.

1583
Shakespeare's first child, Susanna, is born.

1590
Shakespeare's plays start to be peformed.

ABOUT 1587
Shakespeare starts to work in London.

1585
The Shakespeares have twins, Hamnet and Judith.

1592
Plague hits London, killing thousands and forcing playhouses to close to try to stop it spreading.

1593
Shakespeare's name appears in print for the first time on *Venus and Adonis*.

1594
London playhouses reopen; Shakespeare helps found the acting company known as the Lord Chamberlain's Men; they start being invited to perform at court.

1601
The Earl of Essex rebels against the Queen and is beheaded; Shakespeare's father dies and Shakespeare inherits his property.

1599
The rebuilt playhouse opens as the Globe; Will Kemp, the company's clown, quits.

1598
Shakespeare's company loses the lease on the land where their playhouse stands, so they move it.

1603
The old Queen dies and is succeeded by King James; the new King becomes patron of Shakespeare's company, now known as the King's Men, and has them perform often at court.

1607
Shakespeare's eldest daughter, Susanna, marries a Stratford doctor, John Hall.

1611
Shakespeare retires to Stratford.

1613
The Globe burns down after its thatched roof catches fire; it reopens a year later with a tiled roof.

1616
Judith Shakespeare marries a disreputable wine-seller and Shakespeare cuts him out of his will; Shakespeare dies around April 23rd and is buried in Stratford on April 25th.

1623
Shakespeare's f[amily]
put up a monu[ment]
to him; the F[irst]
Folio edition o[f his]
plays is publis[hed]

1578
Shakespeare's father runs into money trouble.

1582
Shakespeare marries Anne Hathaway.

CLOSED

1596
The Lord Chamberlain dies and Shakespeare's company have to find a new patron; the Theatre is closed by the city council; Hamnet Shakespeare dies; the Shakespeare family is granted a coat of arms.

1597
Shakespeare buys New Place, a great house in Stratford, to be his family home.

LIST OF WORKS

Shakespeare wrote at least 37 plays, 154 sonnets and two long poems. We don't have exact dates for when they were written, but experts have worked out rough dates based on performance records and other references.

THE PLAYS

1590-91	The Two Gentlemen of Verona, The Taming of the Shrew
1591-92	Henry VI (Parts 1, 2 and 3)
1592	Titus Andronicus
1592-93	Richard III
1594	The Comedy of Errors
1594-95	Love's Labour's Lost
1595	Richard II, Romeo and Juliet, A Midsummer Night's Dream
1596	King John
1596-97	The Merchant of Venice, Henry IV (Part 1)
1597-98	The Merry Wives of Windsor, Henry IV (Part 2)
1598	Much Ado About Nothing
1598-99	Henry V
1599	Julius Caesar
1599-1600	As You Like It
1600-01	Hamlet, Twelfth Night
1602	Troilus and Cressida
1603	Measure for Measure
1603-04	Othello
1604-05	All's Well That Ends Well
1605	Timon of Athens
1605-06	King Lear
1606	Macbeth, Antony and Cleopatra
1607	Pericles
1608	Coriolanus
1609	The Winter's Tale

THE POEMS

1592-93	Venus and Adonis
1593-94	The Rape of Lucrece
1593-1603	The Sonnets
1603-04	A Lover's Complaint
By 1601	The Phoenix and Turtle

INDEX

ACKNOWLEDGEMENTS

Edited by Jane Chisholm. Art Director: Mary Cartwright.
Photographic manipulation: John Russell.

Cover: detail of fairy (from painting of Titania and Bottom) see credit for pages 16-17; The Globe (about 1598), wood engraving after contemporary drawing © Heritage Images/Corbis; Portrait of Shakespeare, hand-tinted illustration after Martin Droeshout © Bettmann/ Corbis; Map of London (1588) see credit for pages 4-5. Pages 2-3: Shakespeare's Birthplace © Roger de la Harpe/Corbis; Inside the Grammar School © Robert Harding World Imagery/Corbis; Horn-book © Trustees of the British Museum; Anne Hathaway's Cottage © Robert Harding World Imagery/Corbis; New Place Gardens © Greg Balfour Evans/Alamy; Shakespeare Memorial © Colin Underhill/Alamy; Holy Trinity Church © Buddy Mays/Corbis. Pages 4-5: Old St. Paul's, Private Collection/Bridgeman Art Library; Map of London (1588) British Library, London, UK © British Library Board, All Rights Reserved/Bridgeman Art Library; Frost Fair of 1683-84 (c.1685) Yale Center for British Art, Paul Mellon Collection, USA/Bridgeman Art Library; playhouse and ships, two details from View of London by Claes Visscher (1650?) © British Library Board, Maps.162.o.1; Plague Scene, 'God's Tokens' (1625) Private Collection/Bridgeman Art Library. Pages 6-7: Queen Elizabeth at Prayer, from 'Queen Elizabeth's Prayerbook' (1569) © Lambeth Palace Library, London, UK/Bridgeman Art Library; Malvolio and Sir Toby Belch, played by Michael Hordern and Richard Burton, drawn by Ronald Searle for Punch Magazine 13th January 1954 © Punch Limited; Model sailing ship (early 17th century) Ashmolean Museum, University of Oxford, UK/Bridgeman Art Library; Astrological Chart with Signs of the Zodiac (16th century) © Lambeth Palace Library, London, UK/Bridgeman Art Library; Four Humours from 'Quinta Essentia' (pub. 1574) Private Collection/Archives Charmet/Bridgeman Art Library; Fairies from A Midsummer Night's Dream © Bettmann/Corbis. Pages 8-9: Actors at a Village Fair by Cornelis Beelt, Private Collection/Photo © Rafael Valls Gallery, London, UK/Bridgeman Art Library; Will Kemp from Kemp's 'Nine Days Wonder' (pub. 1600) Private Collection/Bridgeman Art Library; Richard Burbage (17th century) © Dulwich Picture Gallery, London, UK/Bridgeman Art Library; First Folio © Nathan Benn/Corbis. Pages 10-11: Penny coin © Trustees of the British Museum; Acting a Shakespeare Play from 'Cassell's Illustrated History of England' (19th century) Private Collection/Stapleton Collection/ Bridgeman Art Library; Queen Elizabeth I playing the Lute by Nicholas Hilliard, Berkeley Castle, Gloucestershire, UK/Bridgeman Art Library; Henry Carey, detail from Procession of the Knights of the Garter at Windsor, print by Marcus Gheeraerts the Elder (1576), British Museum, London, UK/Bridgeman Art Library; Great Hall at Hampton Court Palace © Historical Picture Archive/Corbis; King James I (The Lyte Jewel) © Trustees of the British Museum; Memorial from Poet's Corner, Westminster Abbey, London, UK/Photo: James Brittain/ Bridgeman Art Library; Shakespeare's coat of arms, Art Archive/College of Arms/Eileen Tweedy. Pages 12-13: Swan Theatre (1596) Private Collection/Stapleton Collection/Bridgeman Art Library; Globe Theatre, 1616 (watercolour) © Gallery Collection/Corbis; Shakespeare's Globe © Eric Nathan/Loop Images/Corbis. Pages 14-15: Choosing the Red and White Roses in the Temple Garden by Henry Payne (1910) Houses of Parliament, Westminster, London, UK/Bridgeman Art Library; Portrait of Richard III (c.1480-1500) Royal Collection © 2011 Her Majesty Queen Elizabeth II/Bridgeman Art Library; Kevin Spacey as Richard III (photo) © Evi Filaktou/EPA/Corbis; Henry V (movie still) © John Springer Collection/Corbis; Battle of Agincourt from 'St. Alban's Chronicle' (1415) © Lambeth Palace Library, London, UK/Bridgeman Art Library; Tower of London from 'A Book of the Prospects of the Remarkable Places in and about the City of London' (c.1700) O'Shea Gallery, London, UK/Bridgeman Art Library. Pages 16-17: Midsummer Night's Dream title page © British Library Board; Puck illustration by Arthur Rackham (1908) Private Collection/Stapleton Collection/Bridgeman Art Library; Much Ado About Nothing (movie still) © Pictorial Press Ltd/ Alamy; Twelfth Night, Malvolio played by Stephen Fry (photo) © Robbie Jack/Corbis; Titania and Bottom © Christie's Images/Bridgeman Art Library; Rosalind in the Forest by John Everett Millais (c.1868) © Walker Art Gallery, National Museums Liverpool/Bridgeman Art Library. Pages 18-19: Troilus and Cressida (photo) © Robbie Jack/Corbis; Greek vase depicting Trojan War (c.540 BC) National Gallery of Victoria, Melbourne, Australia/Felton Bequest/Bridgeman Art Library; All's Well That Ends Well (photo) © Robbie Jack/Corbis; Claudio and Isabella by William Holman Hunt (19th century) © Makins Collection/Bridgeman Art Library; Illustration from Merchant of Venice by Christian August Printz (c.1900) Private Collection/Archives Charmet/Bridgeman Art Library. Pages 20-21: Poems title page © Shannon Stapleton/ Reuters/Corbis; Venus and Adonis by Georges Barbier © Stapleton Collection/Corbis; Henry Wriothesley, Earl of Southampton by Nicholas Hilliard (c.1594) Fitzwilliam Museum, University of Cambridge, UK/Bridgeman Art Library; Portrait of a Lady by Nicholas Hilliard (c.1593) © Victoria and Albert Museum, London/V&A Images, All rights reserved; 'Romeo and Juliet' postcard with painting by Jennie Harbour © Mary Evans Picture Library; Shakespeare's Sonnette © Tim Brakemeier/EPA/Corbis. Pages 22-23: Romeo and Juliet by Ford Madox Brown (1868-71) Private Collection/Photo © Christie's Images/Bridgeman Art Library; Ballet of Romeo and Juliet (photo) © Elliott Franks/ArenaPAL www.arenapal.com; Othello (photo) Johan Persson/ArenaPAL www.arenapal.com; Cordelia comforting her father, King Lear, in prison by George William Joy (1886) Leeds Museums and Galleries (Leeds Art Gallery) UK/Bridgeman Art Library; Cleopatra (bas relief) De Agostini Picture Library/G. Dagli Orti/Bridgeman Art Library. Pages 24-25: Hamlet title page © Lebrecht Music and Arts Photo Library/Alamy; Hamlet played by David Tennant (photo) © Robbie Jack/Corbis; Ophelia by Arthur Hughes (1852) Manchester Art Gallery, UK/Bridgeman Art Library; Macbeth poster, Art Archive/Theatre Museum, London/V&A Images; Death of Caesar by Vincenzo Camuccini (19th century) Private Collection/Bridgeman Art Library; Roman coin © Trustees of the British Museum. Pages 26-27: Illustration of the Shipwreck from The Tempest by Edmund Dulac, first published in the U.K. by Hodder Children's, an Imprint of Hachette Children's Books, 338 Euston Road, London NW1 3BH © Christie's Images/Bridgeman Art Library; Storm from The Winter's Tale © Christie's Images/Bridgeman Art Library; Florizel and Perdita © Bonhams, London, UK/Bridgeman Art Library; Miranda © Maas Gallery, London/Bridgeman Art Library; Prospero played by Ralph Fiennes (photo) Marilyn Kingwill/ArenaPAL www.arenapal.com; Ariel from The Tempest (engraving) by Henry Courtney Selous, Private Collection © Look and Learn/Bridgeman Art Library. Pages 28-29: Indian Kathkali-style performance of King Lear © Robbie Jack/Corbis; Throne of Blood movie poster (1957) Toho/Kobal Collection; Five Genuine Autographs of William Shakespeare (engraving) Private Collection/Bridgeman Art Library; Shakepeare jubilee ticket (1769) Art Archive/Garrick Club; Cobbe Portrait (thought to show Shakespeare, from about 1612) © Corbis.

First published in 2015 by Usborne Publishing Ltd.,
Usborne House, 83-85 Saffron Hill, London EC1N 8RT, England. www.usborne.com
Copyright © 2015, 2013 Usborne Publishing Ltd. UE.

All rights reserved. No part of this publication may be reproduced, stored in ___ ___ system or transmit___
or by any means, electronic, mechanical, photocopying, recording or otherw___ ___ prior perm___
The name ___ the devices ♀♈♔ are Trade Ma___ ___ ___blishin___

Usborne Publishing is ___